W9-AJM-094

MAY THE FORCE BE WITH US, PLEASE

A FoxTrot Collection
by Bill Amend

WITHDRAWN

Andrews and McMeel
A Universal Press Syndicate Company
Kansas City

102467

EAU CLAIRE DISTRICT LIBRARY

FoxTrot is distributed internationally by Universal Press Syndicate.

May the Force Be With Us, Please copyright © 1994 by Bill Amend. All rights reserved. Printed in the United States of America. No part of this book may be used or reproduced in any manner whatsoever without written permission except in the case of reprints in the context of reviews. For information write Andrews and McMeel, a Universal Press Syndicate Company, 4900 Main Street, Kansas City, Missouri 64112.

ISBN: 0-8362-1741-1

Library of Congress Catalog Card Number: 93-74264

Printed on recycled paper.

──────── ATTENTION: SCHOOLS AND BUSINESSES ────────

Andrews and McMeel books are available at quantity discounts for bulk purchase for educational, business, or sales promotional use. For information, please write to Special Sales Department, Andrews and McMeel, 4900 Main Street, Kansas City, Missouri 64112.

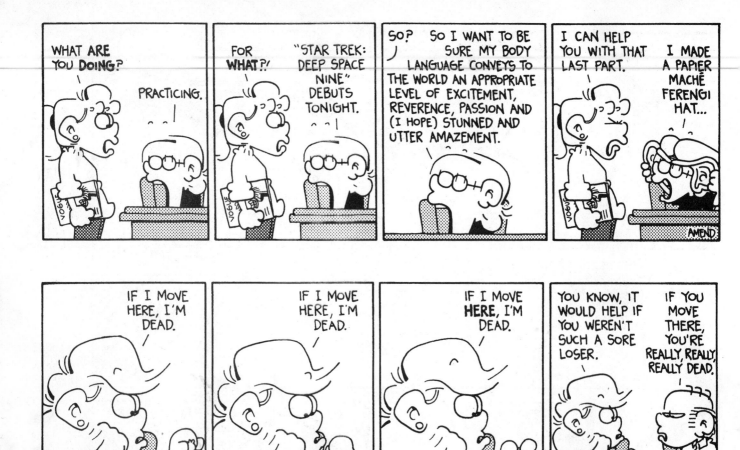

13

EAU CLAIRE DISTRICT LIBRARY

15

THIS JUST ISN'T MY DAY.

18

FoxTrot
BILL AMEND

20

23

FoxTrot
BILL AMEND

27

29

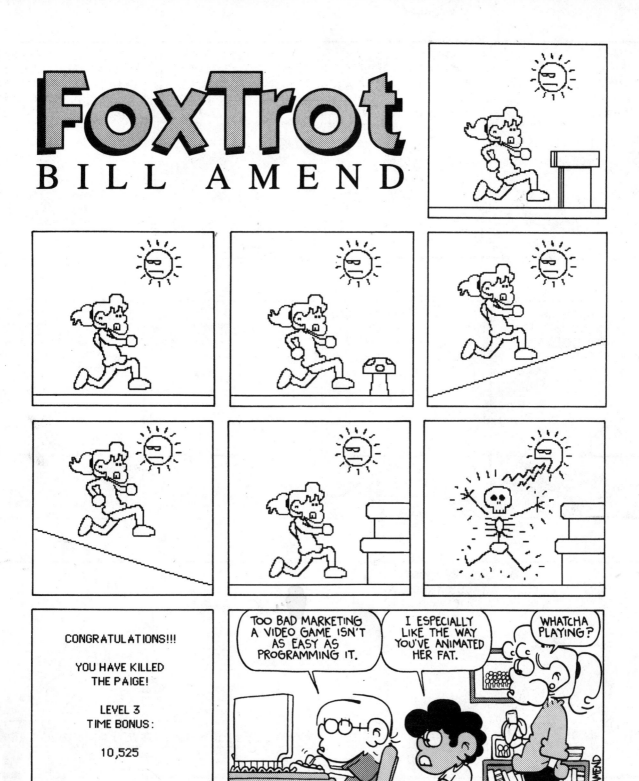

FoxTrot
BILL AMEND

44

45

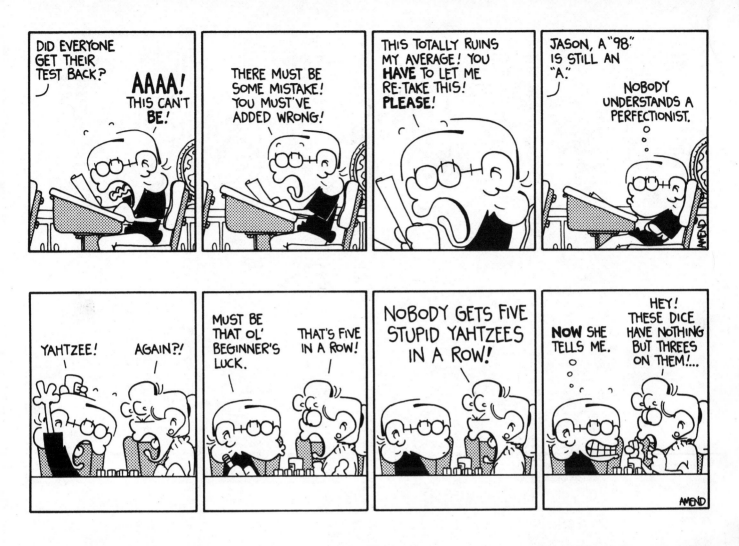

47

50

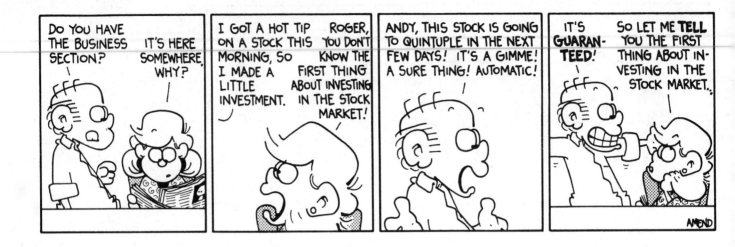

61

62

FoxTrot
BILL AMEND

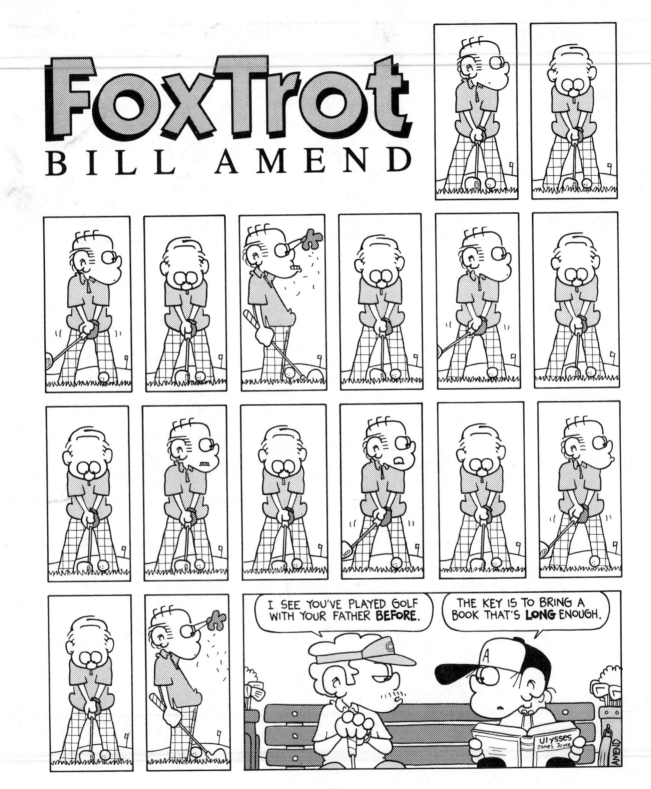

71

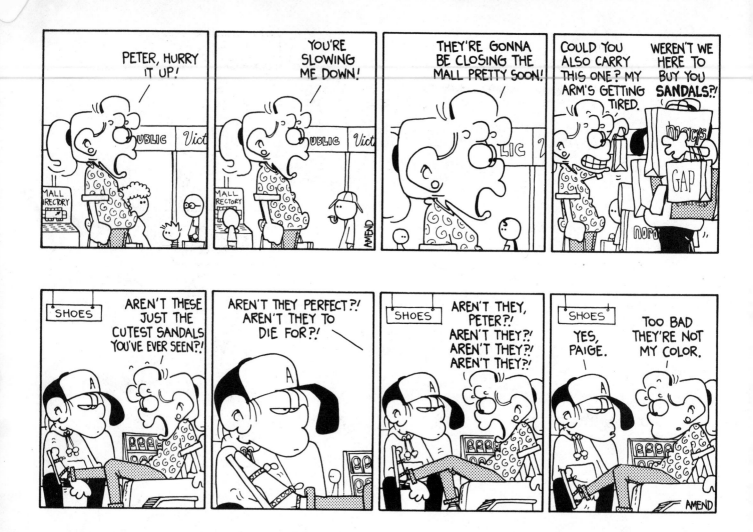

89

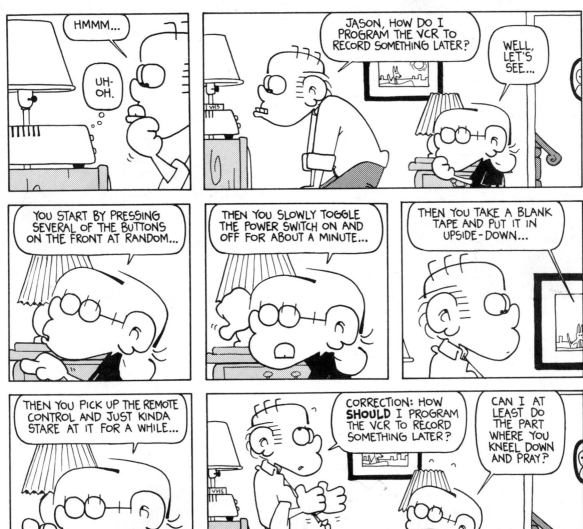

92

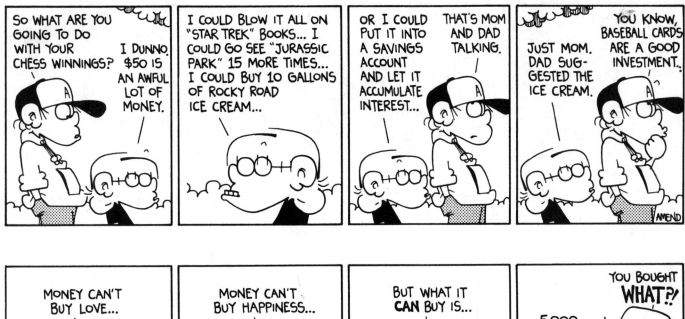

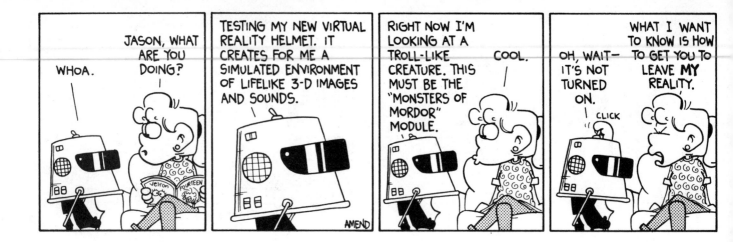

99

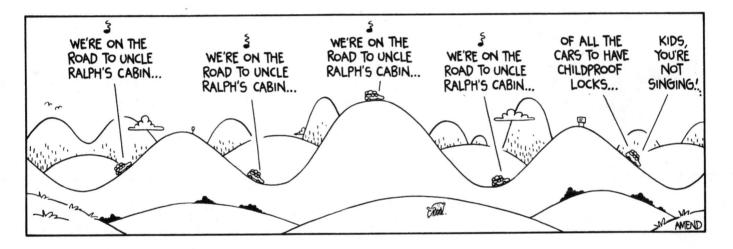

107

108

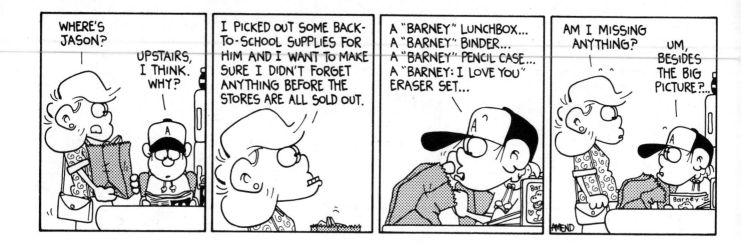

FoxTrot
BILL AMEND

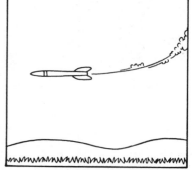

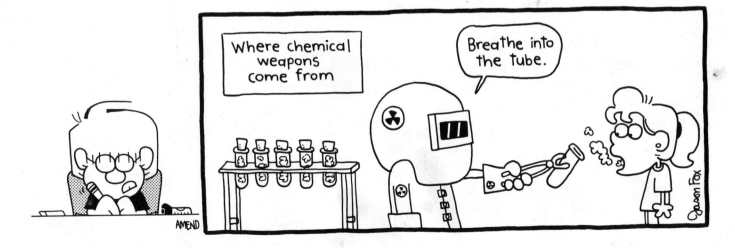

116

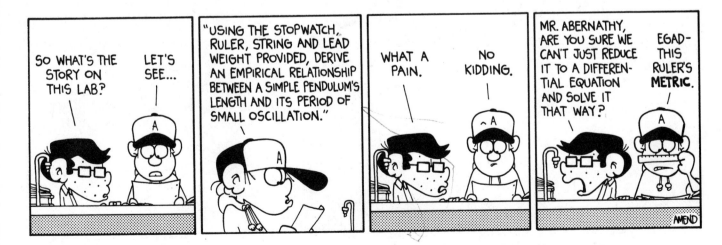

120

121

123

125

EAU CLAIRE DISTRICT LIBRARY